Freedom Now

A Non-Violent Conservative Revolution Removing America's Leftist Ruling Elites Restoring Constitutional Government

James Ronald Kennedy

Foreword by Walter Donald Kennedy

Wake Forest, NC
www.scuppernongpress.com

Freedom Now
A Non-Violent Conservative Revolution Removing America's
Leftist Ruling Elites Restoring Constitutional Government
By James R. Kennedy

©2022 The Scuppernong Press

First Printing

The Scuppernong Press
PO Box 1724
Wake Forest, NC 27588
www.scuppernongpress.com

Cover and book design by Frank B. Powell, III

International Standard Book Number
ISBN 978-1-942806-44-8

Library of Congress Control Number: 2022908954

Contents

Freedom Now: A Non-Violent Conservative Revolution

Foreword

As Americans were approaching Easter weekend, 2022, the news media was buzzing with stories about Florida's so-called, "Don't say Gay" law. Although the word "Gay" is nowhere to be found in the law, the progressive, woke, establishment used this false narrative to ridicule Florida's legislation. This law prevents adults from teaching homosexual/transgender ideology to children, K through the third grade. At one time in America, any adult who approached a stranger's child with overtly sexual messages would be called a "pervert" and suffer the consequences. But not in today's America!

When Alabama passed a law similar to Florida's law, the Federal government put Alabama on notice that the full weight of the Federal government would be used to overturn the democratic wishes of the people of Alabama. The same supreme and indivisible Federal government threatening Alabama is the same Federal government that sent Federal Marshals into Alabama courthouses and forcefully removed copies of the Ten Commandments. It should be noted that these two actions were committed by a federal administration from not just one political party but by administrations from both national political parties!

While the United States is spending billions of dollars defending national borders from Korea to Ukraine, our national borders go virtually unprotected. Presently, America is facing one of the world's greatest immigration invasions. Although willing to use this crisis to build political support, neither political party is willing to fix the problem. Many Americans were incensed when, during the Obama Administration, free cell phones were given welfare recipients. Currently, the Biden Administration is perusing a policy of giving free cell phones to illegal immigrants!

The "take away" message for Americans is that America has, as General Robert E. Lee warned, become "aggressive abroad and despotic at home." Can America be saved from this repugnant condition? Yes, as is pointed out in chapter eight of this booklet, there is an answer. It is strong medicine but life-threatening maladies demand strong medicine. Will America take the medicine and live or, like a spoil child, reject the cure?

— *Walter Donald Kennedy*

Introduction:

Confronting the Potential of Freedom
with
Truth and Courage

If we are honest with ourselves, if we listen to that still small voice within, we will admit that, as a people, we ignore the potential of true American freedom. We ignore the potential to reclaim the freedom taken from us. The potential is always there. There's the potential, so what are you supposed to do with it? How do you confront this potential? You confront it with truth and courage. With the power of truth and courage, you transform potential into what it can be — into reality. You change your current dismal, politically correct, Woke world into a better place — maybe not a perfect place but one a lot better than the one we suffer under today! Now that's your job, your responsibility. In Genesis, God confronts potential and produces something that did not exist, and He says: "it is good." Each time God confronts potential and creates something new, He says: "it is good." There is a lesson to be learned in these scriptures. It instructs us that when we confront potential with truth and courage, we produce something good. It is not easy for man to be courageous, but if you confront potential with truth and courage, you will produce something good. This is our challenge — we who understand the truth must be the ones who confront the potential of a better world, the potential of producing a better society — one eminently better than the Woke, politically correct, neo-Marxist society we suffer under today.

Freedom is out there waiting for us to turn potential into reality. God is on the side of those who love the truth. He will bless those who are courageous enough to confront and defeat evil. The potential of creating a nation in which America's traditional, conservative, moral, and political values are the standard now confronts us. Our challenge is to confront the potential of freedom with truth and courage and turn the potential of freedom into the reality of Freedom!

Deo Vindice

Chapter 1

Creating a Government that Protects and Promotes Traditional American Values

The current Federal Government (Congress, Supreme Court, and the Office of the President)[1] does not protect and promote the interests of average Americans. The United States' current government is radically different from the government America's Founding Fathers created! We are no longer free citizens but mere subjects of a leftist controlled supreme Federal Government. The cur-

We will destroy the leftist ruling elites who now control America. We will defeat them using the new tactics and strategy of Irregular Political Warfare.

rent overgrown, tax, borrow, and spend government with unlimited powers over its subjects is the opposite of what the Founders intended. It is sad and unfortunate that we find ourselves in this position — a situation that is nothing less than political slavery. However, "We the people" have the ability to use the peaceful, non-violent technique of irregular political warfare to overthrow the Deep State's ruling elites in Washington, DC, the Wall Street Globalists, and America's Digital Masters in Silicon Valley. Overthrowing the current, self-serving, leftist, political establishment is an ambitious task, but with the correct tactics and strategy we shall win! "We the people" can defeat our self-appointed masters, destroy their tyrannical political system, and establish a new one based upon liberty. We have the potential to make a fundamental change in the current, left-of-center, political establishment. Using the tactics and strategy outlined in the last chapter, we will make a fundamental change in the Federal Government. But will our new political system that replaces the ruling elite's system be any better than the current one?

What will America's political environment look like after we remove the current corrupt and oppressive political establishment? We owe it to our fellow Americans and the world to make clear what principles our new American government will follow. What will be the major difference between the current, supreme, all powerful, elitists-controlled Federal Government and our new, constitutionally limited, American Republic of Sovereign States? Actually, our "new" government will be similar to America's original, constitutionally limited Republic as establish by America's Founding Fathers.

There are eight major changes that our new American government will make. The first essential change establishes the basic American principle of local self-government. The seven changes that follow the first change flow from the established right of local self-government.

1. Political power will be removed from Washington, DC, and returned to "We the People" within our Sovereign States. Local self-government, enforced by real States' Rights, will trump Federal court orders, regulations, and unconstitutional laws enacted by a left-of-center Congress. (How this fundamental change will be done is explained in Chapter 8).

2. The people of each Sovereign State will decide whether prayer and Bible reading will be allowed in their public schools as well as whether the people will allow the public display of traditional holiday religious symbols.

3. The people of each Sovereign State will decide when human life begins and therefore when and in what manner their state will protect human life.

4. The people of each Sovereign State will have the authority to protect their state from armed or unarmed invasion via secure borders and the right to determine citizenship for those seeking to legally immigrate to our country.

5. The people of each Sovereign State will have the right to determine if state tax payer funds will be used to pay welfare or health benefits to illegal aliens.

6. The people of each Sovereign State will have the power to establish non-arbitrary voting qualifications and to police voting to ensure accurate and legitimate elections.

7. Parents will have ultimate authority to decide what will be taught to their children in tax-supported educational institutions from kindergartens to universities.

8. The Sovereign State will have the power to interpose its Sovereign authority between the Federal Government and any attempt to infringe upon the law-abiding citizen's right to keep and bear arms.

The Founding Fathers created a limited Federal Government, leaving the vast majority of social and political decision to be made by "We the people" at the local level. They created a Republic of Sovereign States that was based upon the concept of local self-government. Our Founding Fathers recognized that one set of cultural, social, or religious norms could not be established for a people with such vast differences in cultural, social, religious, and political attitudes. For example, in 1859, the State of Wisconsin used its Sovereign authority to nullify the Fugitive Slave clause of the U.S. Constitution. When Wisconsin entered the Union, it agreed to abide by the Constitution, which clearly included the Fugitive Slave Clause. Subsequent to its admission to the Union, it became morally reprehensible for the citizens of Wisconsin to aid in the capture and return of run-a-way slaves. The people of Wisconsin used the State's Sovereign authority to halt the enforcement of the Federal Fugitive Slave law within their state. The antagonistic views on slavery were harmonized within the Union by using the American, constitutional principle of state nullification.

In our new American government, the principle of local self-government will be used to harmonize the vast differences between Red States/Red Counties and Blue States/Blue Counties. (Red meaning limited government, typically conservative voting states or counties; Blue meaning big government, typically liberal voting states or counties).

Today an irreconcilable political divide exists in the United States. Those who believe in protecting the life of the unborn will no longer give their consent to being ruled by those who believe they have a right to extinguish the life of an unborn human. There is no compromise between life and death! There can be no harmony between those who want to destroy the Second Amendment's right to keep and bear arms and those of us who want to protect our Second Amendment rights. In essence, there will never be peace between those who insist on a left-ist leaning, big, centralized, supreme, Washington, DC, government and those who insist on a constitutionally limited Federal Government and local self-government. In the current system of the supreme Federal Government, the Blue States/Counties rule over the Red States/Counties. (This is true even when Republicans are in power!) Blue State America, under the current political system of supreme Federalism, can use the force of government to compel Red State America to live under a system that we find morally unacceptable. This situation is, in principle, the same situation the people of Wisconsin were in back in 1859. But back then, they had the right of local self-government via nullification to protect their interests.

We who believe in the right of local self-government are the only ones who have a solution to America's irreconcilable political divide — we offer the only means to harmonize such radical differences within the current United States — thereby preserving these United States as one united country. Otherwise, a division, a national divorce, will occur. "We the people" who honor traditional, American, conservative political and moral[2] values will no longer be ruled by those who hate and seek to dominate us.

For the first time in modern American Political history, we have a solution to America's irreconcilable political divide. "We the people" will either harmonize the Red State/Blue State divide, or else we shall create a Red State-Red County Nation of our own!

Freedom Now: A Non-Violent Conservative Revolution

Chapter 2

Equal Rights Denied to Traditional Conservative Americans

The majority of Americans expects the Federal Government to enforce reasonable immigration laws — yet the Federal Government is actively involved in assisting the breaking of our nation's immigration laws by illegal aliens. Americans do not want to be taxed to support every third world person who illegally crosses our nation's border — yet, the ruling elite in Washington, DC, with the support of their allies in the media, are using our tax dollars to fund welfare and healthcare benefits for illegal immigrants. The majority of Americans support the idea of voter ID — yet, the ruling elite in Washington, DC, and their allies in the media, are vocally opposed to voter ID or any law that would help to guarantee legitimate elections — elections that voters confidently feel the results reflect the actual will of America's voters. Most Americans want their state to make policy decisions about abortion, yet the Federal Government's Supreme Court federalized abortion, thereby forbidding the states from passing laws regulating abortion. The majority of Americans believe in the traditional, Judeo-Christian definition of marriage as between one man and one woman — yet, the Federal Supreme Court forbids the states to enact laws reflecting the will of the people. Most Americans are horrified that a male per-

We have a solution to an oppressive Federal Government that does not represent the political and social interest of average, middle-class Americans.

vert can follow little girls into a public restroom, yet the Federal Supreme Court ruled that such perverts are now a Federally protected minority. The majority of Americans are opposed to the Federal Government sending American youth off to fight no-win wars that only benefit America's military-industrial-complex — yet, flag-draped coffins continue to return home.

The list above could go on and on — Federal agents weaponized against parents who oppose the teaching of Critical Race Theory, Federal IRS weaponized and used to oppress Tea Party leaders, the Federal Government mandating the medicating of Americans with COVID vaccines, inflation, passing laws that encourage Global-ists to move American jobs offshore, national politicians with financial connections to the Chinese Communist Party, Deep State bureaucrats undermining a duly elected President, etc. "We the people" no longer have the Ameri-can government our Founding Fathers created! The Deep State's ruling elite and their corrupt political allies dis-torted and perverted America's government. But "We the people" will set matters straight!

America's traditional moral, social, and political values are based upon Judeo-Christian moral teachings, which stress the importance of the individual. Individual respon-sibility and individual accountability go hand-in-hand with individual rights. Group grievances and group rights are neo-Marxist inventions used to divide, dominate, and eventually destroy our society. The reason America's Woke, politically correct establishment opposes Christian moral values is because Western Christian civilization stresses the value of the individual. In the West, the importance of the individual, as opposed to the group, allowed for the development and over time, the refinement of democratic institutions that support individual freedom. Neo-Marxists hate Western Christian civilization because it makes a mockery of their death-producing, hate-filled, leftist ideology.

Classical Marxism falsely claimed that there is a natural conflict between the haves and the have-nots of society. According to Marxist ideology, this supposed conflict is the source of societies' inequities. Marxist ideology views the individual as nothing, while the group is everything. Marx saw society as an ever-increasing conflict between the rich (bourgeoisie) and the poor (the proletariat).[3] Classical Marxism viewed society as a conflict between two major groups, the owners of businesses and the workers. By the late 1950s, "intellectuals" who were followers of Marxism (especially French intellectuals such as Derrida and Foucault)[4] unexpectedly, and to their great disappointment, realized the failure of their cherished Marxist ideology in the Soviet Union and Communist China. But they and other ideological Marxists were not willing to admit the failure of their pet ideology. They refused to reject their cherished ideology even though history and over 100 million dead humans proved Marxism to be an utter, devastating, and malignant failure. They salvaged classical Marxism by transforming it into neo-Marxism. As neo-Marxists, they modified classical Marxism by describing society not as a struggle between business owners and workers but as a struggle between groups. Neo-Marxists claim Western Christian society is based upon a power struggle between white males (the oppressive and evil patriarchy)[5] and all other groups. These "other groups" include blacks and other non-whites, women, sexual perverts as defined by traditional Christian moral teachings, etc. Neo-Marxists view society as controlled by the patriarchy (white males), who are the universal oppressors, and all other groups who are victims of the patriarchy.

America's Woke, politically correct society results from the victory of neo-Marxist ideology in education, media, and the status quo political establishment in Washington, DC.[6] The sad reality is that the Woke, politically correct establishment in Washington, DC, has major influence, if not total control, not only in Washington, DC, but they also control or influence local political leaders, civic and social institutions, large corporate boards of directors, and, sadly, many churches and other religious institutions, such as seminaries.

In Woke America — Some Americans are "more equal" than others

Woke or Politically Correct America is an out-growth of neo-Marxist influence and control of America's institutions of influence. America's colleges and universities are dominated by an academic neo-Marxism ideology known as postmodernism. "We the people" who believe in traditional, conservative, American values are forced by "our" government to pay taxes that finance the leftist, anti-American indoctrination of our children and grand-children. This leftist indoctrination begins in the universities and flows through the entire educational system down to kindergarten. Public education has become public propaganda promoting leftist, neo-Marxist ideas. The digital and mainline media are outspoken supporters of the neo-Marxist ideology of group rights and group grievances against traditional America. The impact of just these two agents of influence (universities and the media) is demonstrated by the fact that a majority of "conservative" Americans self-censor their speech to avoid being labeled as racist, white supremacist, homophobe, or misogynist. For instance, if an individual dare points out that America's gun violence is not a result of law-abiding Americans owning fire arms but primarily due to black criminals and gang-bangers freely operating in Democratic-controlled cities. The facts are there, and the data is clear, but woe unto he who is brave enough to point out these facts! Our First Amendment Right of Free Speech is shut down not by government but by neo-Marxist agents of influence in education and the media — especially the digital media. Their influence — their power to intimidate — extends into corporate America as evidenced by Woke companies that punish violations of politically correct speech codes and endless demands for more affirmative action or diversity in the workplace. In America today, freedom of speech is permitted only if you are speaking according to the leftists, neo-Marxist party line. Leftist Americans are "more equal" than traditional, conservative Americans.

One of the great themes of American government is the idea that "all men are created equal." As originally written in the Declaration of Independence, this "equality" meant equal before the law and God. Thomas Jefferson understood that no man is born booted and spurred to ride over other men.[7] While traditional, conservative Americans believe in equality before the law, our neo-Marxist opponents believe that only those who follow leftist ideology should receive government protection. Recall the massive number of riots and killings that occurred in 2019 to 2020 with little, if any, efforts to identify and prosecute those involved. Why? Because they were part the neo-Marxist storm troopers fighting to advance the neo-Marxist revolution. Now compare the reaction of America's political establishment when they were confronted by relatively peaceful protestors on January 6, 2022. Leftist protestors are "more equal" than conservative protestors.

America's political establishment has one set of rules

for "conservatives" and another for leftist politicians and bureaucrats. Leftist Lois Lerner, while holding a high Federal office in the IRS, spent a great deal of time and effort harassing conservative Tea Party members. Eventually, she was accused of intentionally destroying official IRS records, but she was never investigated and punished. What would happen to a conservative who destroys records needed by the IRS? Deep State bureaucrats are "more equal" than average Americans.

Deep State bureaucrats spent millions of taxpayer dollars "investigating" the false claim that President Trump conspired with Russia, yet they refuse to investigate Hillary Clinton's campaign involvement in the fake Trump/Russia connection used to harass a duly elected president during his entire term as president. They also carefully avoid investigating Washington politicians of both national political parties with significant financial connections to Communist China. Leftist-ruling elites, and their Republican "lap dogs," are "more equal" than the average American. America's ruling elites get to select which laws they obey and which laws they enforce.

It should be obvious to all by now that "We the people" do not enjoy equal rights under the current corrupt and unconstitutional political system. We are, in fact, second class people — we are no longer citizens in a Constitutional Republic, but we are subjects to the neo-Marxist-controlled supreme Federal Government.

"We the people" have become political slaves in our own country.
But
A slave revolt is building!

Freedom Now: A Non-Violent Conservative Revolution

Chapter 3

The Sad Reality of Political Slavery

Americans find it difficult to accept that, in today's leftist political system, traditional, conservative Americans do not have a government that consistently protects, and, more importantly, promotes their values and interests. The Deep State in Washington, DC, the Globalists on Wall Street, and anti-free speech oligarchs of Silicon Valley have the supreme Federal Government to protect and promote their interests, but "We the people" have no such government! America's leftist ruling elites get political results while we get, at best, rhetoric — hot speeches made for home consumption.

Counterfeit-conservatives elected by conservative voters **NEVER** have offered a real solution to the unconstitutional, out-of-control, system of supreme federalism. They, especially Republicans, cannot find the courage to identify the essential cause of today's failed system of Washington, DC's centralized, all-powerful, government. They refuse to acknowledge that local self-government is impossible under the current system of government — the system of supreme Federalism. "We the people" have the appearance of self-government, but we **do not** have the final say-so about how our communities will be governed. Republicans cannot admit that their party was key in destroying America's original, legitimate, constitutionally limited Republic of Sovereign States and its replacement with the current unconstitutional and therefore illegitimate supreme Federal Government.[8] Republican leaders worship the Party more than the truth and they viciously slander anyone who dares to confront them with the truth about their Party and the destruction of

America's original and legitimate constitutionally limited Republic of Sovereign States!

Freedom is seldom lost all at once. Free people do not wake up one day to find themselves enslaved to an oppressive government. In most cases, freedom is not lost all at once but gradually. If the Federal Government in 1960 declared that whites are guilty of systemic racism, and therefore, whites must meekly accept enforced discrimination against all whites to make up for the alleged sins of the past — a conservative revolution would have occurred. Every politician who supported such oppressive ideas would have been thrown out of office. Yet, today, the Federal Government uses the power of government to enforce what was once called affirmative action but today goes under the, seemingly harmless, Woke or politically correct banner of "diversity," or "equity." In 1962-3, when the Federal Supreme Court outlawed prayer and Bible reading in public schools, if the Federal Supreme Court, at the same time, declared transgenders to be a protected minority and ordered Christians to bake wedding cakes for homosexual couples, an anti-supreme Federal Government revolution would have occurred. It did not happen because neo-Marxists are experts in the art of social and political gradualism. They silently infiltrated America's institutions of influence and eventually took control of those institutions. They acted slowly, quietly, and behind the scene, while "We the people" went about our daily lives totally unaware of the chains of political slavery that were gradually being fixed upon us. "We the people" became slaves to the neo-Marxist political establishment without realizing it.

America's Founding Fathers understood the dangers of political slavery and were very jealous of their freedom. They would not allow the slightest encroachment upon their freedoms to go unchallenged. Our Founding Fathers understood that the first small step of encroachment upon the people's rights is just the precursor to the next and even more oppressive step. America's Founding Fathers understood that once such oppressive steps started, it would be hard to stop, much less reverse. In 1776, they initiated their revolution against political slavery.

George Washington argued that the mother country's King and Parliament "are endeavoring by every piece of Art and despotism to fix the Shackles of Slavery upon us."[9] John Dickinson of Pennsylvania (1732-1808) was a reluctant Revolutionary, but he knew free people could lose their freedom and become political slaves when "the mad moment which slipt [slipped] upon them the shackles of slavery."[10] The

We shall use irregular political warfare to break the chains of political slavery that bind us to the current unconstitutional leftist government — a despotic government controlled by self-appointed ruling elites.

American Revolution (1776-1783) was a revolt against the King's gradual efforts to violate the "rights of Englishmen" in America. The King and Parliament's violation of the ancient rights of Englishmen and the central government in London's slow but steady encroachment upon rights belonging to free men caused Englishmen in America to become "Rebels!" America's Patriots realize that, if such gradual encroachments continued, Americans would become political slaves to the central government in England. The American Colonies fought the War for American Independence because they would rather risk death than become political slaves to a big, oppressive, supreme, central government in London.

America's Founding Fathers set the standard for us. It is now time for us to do our children and future generations of Americans a great favor — *we must abolish political slavery in our country!* The following are a few examples of how the neo-Marxist-controlled central government in Washington, DC, turned formerly free Americans into the Federal Government's political slaves:

- Biden's Department of Homeland Security issued a heightened terrorist threat assessment centered around "online misinformation" targeting opponents of the Biden Administration. Conservative taxpayers are funding this Federal effort.
- This national security assessment came just days after the Biden White House called on audio streaming giant Spotify to do more to censor Joe Rogan and others who would dare deviate from the government-approved Covid narrative.
- The Biden White House uses the Department of Homeland Security to amplify its crusade against prohibited speech. This is a dangerous assault on the First Amendment. Political slaves have no recourse other than to meekly accept the efforts of their masters to censor their right to free speech.
- Two Democrats on the Senate Intelligence Committee say the CIA has a secret, undisclosed data repository that includes information collected about Americans. This is a violation of the Constitution's Fourth Amendment right "to be secure in their persons, houses, papers, and effects, against unreasonable searches." Who is paying for the spying on Americans? America's political slaves are paying!
- U. S. Attorney General, Garland, allegedly mobilized the FBI to track parents who made critical comments

about school board members. According to the *New York Post*, a whistleblower revealed that the FBI created a "threat tag" for parents. The supreme Federal Government's Deep State uses our tax dollars to turn the FBI into an American KGB or Gestapo.

- President Joe Biden's massive release of illegal aliens into the United States interior will cost American taxpayers at least $6.6 billion **annually**. The neo-Marxist political elite in Washington, DC, don't care about the cost because they know America's political slaves will pay it.

Political slavery is never removed by begging or compromising with the political masters who control ultimate power. Power can only be countered by power! "We the people" will gain political power by diligently applying the tactics and strategy of irregular political warfare. We shall give our neo-Marxist oppressors a fight they have never faced!

In the Spirit of 1776 — the time for a nonviolent, peaceful slave revolt is NOW!

Freedom Now!

Chapter 4

Congress no Longer Represents
Average Americans

Middle-class, conservative, Americans have no actual (effective and real) representation in Congress! This is true regardless of who we elect to Congress. The primary purpose of government in a free society is to protect and promote the interests of the people. Far from protecting and promoting the interests of middle-class Americans, politicians in Congress generally ignore the interests of "We the people" while catering to the interests of well financed lobbyists and other special interest groups.

Each member of the House of Representatives "represents" approximately 700,000 people. The interests of unorganized individuals mean nothing when compared to the interests of well-paid corporate lobbyists and social justice, neo-Marxist pressure groups such as Black Lives Matter, the NAACP, or the Southern Poverty Law Center. Corporate lobbyists have bags of cash and promises of cushy positions on Corporate Boards for any elected official who will vote in favor of corporate interests. Organized interest overrules the interests of 700,000 unorganized individuals back in the Congressman's Congressional district. This is one of the major reasons why "conservative" politicians refuse to protect and promote traditional, conservative, American moral, social, and political values. Counterfeit-conservative poli-

We shall use our political power to close the gap between the promises of elected conservatives and conservative results.

ticians generally "talk the talk," but they seldom, if ever, "walk the walk." There is a great gap between conservative rhetoric in Congress and conservative results in Congress!

"Conservative" politicians refuse to actively protect and promote our interests because of fear. They fear the loss of almost unending personal financial benefits from corporate lobbyists, and they fear being slandered by the neo-Marxists controlled media. They know that the neo-Marxist media will label them white supremacists, racists, homophobes, misogynists, etc., if the "conservative" politician dares to stand-up for traditional American conservative moral or political values. Such controversy would hinder the "conservative" politician's re-election prospects. And never forget that, in the current system of government, the politician's primary concern is to get in office and then to remain in office. Therefore, "conservative" politicians avoid controversial topics — topics that might bring down the wrath of the neo-Marxist media and pressure groups on our "conservative" politicians. This corrupted system of elitist government works well for those in league with the ruling elite. Never forget that our "conservative" elected officials are either an active or passive part of the ruling elite.

The majority of elected members of the United States Congress are millionaires. How can millionaires represent the interests of average men and women? Millionaires do not feel the financial stress caused by an increase in the price of food, gasoline, or building supplies. But unrepresented, middle-class Americans do feel the pinch of high taxation and inflation. The median net worth (assets minus liabilities) of Americans in 2020 was $121,760. Contrast this with the millionaires in Congress who pass laws "We the people" must obey. The Speaker of the House (2020), Democrat Nancy Pelosi, saw her wealth increase from $41 million in 2004 to $115 million in 2020. Senate Minority Leader (2020), Republican Mitch McConnell, managed to increase his wealth during that same time from $3 million to $34 million. The ability of members of Congress to increase their wealth is demonstrated by Representative Collin Peterson, Democrat from Minnesota. Representative Peterson began his career as a Federal "public servant" in 2008 with a worth of around $123,500, and by 2020, his "hard work" increased his worth to $4.2 million.[11] Not a bad gig if you can get it!

During 2003-09, Republicans such as Bob Dole and John McCain used their influence to get a Russian "gangster" capitalist, Deripaska, a visa to come to the United States. Initially, the FBI denied his request, but after consultation with U.S. Senators, the FBI relented and allowed the "Kremlin-tied" Russian "gangster" to enter the U.S.[12] Lobbyists do not work for free and they do not work to protect and promote the interests of average Americans. But national politicians of both parties and Deep State bureaucrats find the current system of government very lucrative — no wonder they work so hard to keep their system of government intact.

Even worse than the corruption is that many in Congress are "in the tank for the Chinese Communist Party!" The average American has credible suspicions that COVID 19 originated in a Chinese Communist Party research lab. But for some reason, Congress refused to investigate the origins of the Chinese virus. Why? Peter Schweizer, author of *Red-Handed: How American Elites Get Rich Helping China Win* explained why:

Look, Nancy Pelosi's family has done a lot of business in China since the COVID outbreak. She has refused to allow a single congressional hearing to even discuss the origins of the COVID virus.[13]

Republicans are just as involved as Democrats! Republican leader in the Senate, Mitch McConnell, and his wife became multimillionaires primarily due to their connections with Communist China.[14] A recent article exposed 23 former U.S. Senators and Congressmen who lobbied for various Chinese military or Chinese intelligence-linked companies after they retired from government service. The majority were Republican! Under America's current political system, the ruling elite are working for their benefit while "We the people" are forced to accept oppressive and economically devastating edicts, rules, regulations, laws, and taxes passed by the rich ruling elite in Washington, DC.

"We the people" cannot depend solely upon electing good conservatives and hoping that the Republican Party will control Congress and protect our interests. For example, recently, 22 Republicans signed on to a bill sponsored by Republican Stewart of Utah. His bill would make sexual orientation and gender identity a federally protected class.[15] The leftist Federal EEOC (Equal Employment Opportunity Commission) would have a field-day enforcing this bill if it were passed. His bill went nowhere in 2019, but he reintroduced it in 2021. The fact that 22 so-called "conservative" Republicans signed on to support the bill should tell average Americans just how untrustworthy elected Republicans can be. They are part of the political status quo. Their primary purpose is to maintain their positions where they enjoy the perks, privileges, profits, and power of an elected member of the ruling elite.

America's "representative democracy" died when the Federal Government became the supreme authority in America. It died when "We the people" no longer had the authority of our Sovereign State to stand between our rights and liberty and an oppressive, elitist controlled supreme Federal Government. The time has come for Americans to realize that Congress does not represent America's middle-class. "We the people" have become political slaves! Under the current system of elitists-controlled government — Congress no longer represents the interests of average Americans!

America's Colonial Patriots refused to allow their central government to tax and rule them without representation. "We the people" no longer have real representation in Congress. A peaceful slave revolt is developing!

Freedom Now: A Non-Violent Conservative Revolution

Chapter 5

The Supreme Court's Assault on America's Traditional Values

The United States Supreme Court is an active opponent of America's traditional, conservative moral and political values. In a relatively recent court case, the United States Supreme Court made male sexual perverts calling themselves transgenders a Federally protected minority.[16] One commentator noted the Supreme Court's new definition of "sex," which now includes sexual orientation or gender identity, will create a flood of new leftwing lawsuits. Of primary concern is leftist lawsuits against churches. This followed a previous case in which the United States Supreme Court declared the Defense of Marriage Act, passed by Congress, unconstitutional, thereby giving same-sex marriage equal status with traditional marriage. This decision of the Federal Supreme Court prohibited states from defining marriage. Under our current, unconstitutional, system of supreme Federalism, States' Rights exist only when allowed by the supreme Federal Government — in fact, States' Rights no longer exist! What we have today is States' Privileges. Slaves enjoy "privileges" only if their master allows it.

Our Conservative Revolution is the only peaceful solution to a Supreme Court that does not honor the limitations imposed by the original Constitution.

These rulings are part of what former Federal Judge Robert Bork described as America's progressive "slouching toward Gomorrah." The attack against traditional Judeo-

Christian moral values began in the early 1960s when the United States Supreme Court threw God, prayer, and Bible reading out of our public schools. The only voice to descent that Supreme Court decision was Justice Potter Stewart. He warned that what the U.S. Supreme Court did with its anti-traditional values ruling was to replace traditional Judeo-Christian values with "a religion of secularism." Who are these nine elitist, unelected, black-robed men and women who sit in judgment on, and ultimately establishes, our communities' social and political norms?

All Supreme Court Justices enter the ruling elite by first obtaining a liberal education at an elite, ideologically leftist university. A recent study demonstrated that only 15 percent of professors teaching in law schools were conservative. It also indicated approximately 65 percent of America's lawyers were liberal.[17] This is no surprise when you consider that only one out of twenty law schools was considered conservative. Your tax dollars at work, either through tax-support of public universities or tax supported Federal education loans. "We the people" are being forced to provide the tax dollars that are used to pay leftist professors and universities to indoctrinate (brainwash) our children and grandchildren.

In September of 2018, a Federal Court issued a ruling in *Martin v. Boise* that Federalized homelessness. In the ruling, the Federal Court denied the right of local self-government by rejecting the city's right to regulate homeless encampments in public places. The ruling stated that a city could not ban camping in public places if it did not provide enough homeless beds for the homeless population. The United States Supreme Court, in 2019, refused to hear the city's appeal, thus creating a legal precedent that stands today. If you ever wondered how and why our city's streets, parks, sidewalks, and overpasses became camping grounds for the homeless — now you know. The rights and liberties — including our safety — of "We the people" are insignificant if they do not conform to Woke, politically correct, neo-Marxist ideology. So much for our inherent right of local self-government. But local self-government is not part of the Federal Court's legal doctrine — it is replaced by the rule of leftist elites in Washington, DC.

In 2020, a judge in Wisconsin ordered the expenditure of taxpayer dollars to fund sex reassignment surgery for a man jailed for raping his ten-year-old daughter! A Federal District Judge ordered the once sovereign state of Wisconsin to house the male prisoner in a women's prison while he was awaiting his taxpayer-funded sex-change surgery.[18] This is just one more example of the Federal Government's judicial system pushing our society further down the road toward Gomorrah.

Below are a few examples of how far-removed elitists Federal Courts have become and how far removed the Feds are from the common sense enjoyed by most Americans:

- A Federal Court upheld the EPA's (Environmental Protection Agency) effort to take over a farmer's land because the EPA held that it was "wetlands."[19] Some described this new constitutional theory as the "glancing geese" theory because any land, regardless of its owner, becomes Federal wetlands if a flight of geese could glance down and see water on private land.
- The Federal Supreme Court blocks President Trump's efforts to have census data identify if the individual is an American citizen. "Conservative" Justice Roberts joined the four liberal Justices in the 5-4 decision.[20]
- In the middle of the Chinese COVID pandemic,

a federal judge ordered the once sovereign state of Florida to release hundreds of illegal immigrants.[21]

- Federal Supreme Court upholds order to close church services during the pandemic. "Conservative" Chief Justice Roberts joined the four liberal Justices in ruling that churches and other religious gatherings were not "essential" even though the order allowed supermarkets, stores, hair salons, and marijuana dispensaries to remain open.[22] So much for Freedom of Religion in modern leftist controlled America.

- Most have forgotten about the Federal Supreme Court's infamous forced bussing decision. In 1971, the Supreme Court ruled the Federal Government had the constitutional right to deny parents the right to choose the public school their children would attend.[23] Nothing did more to destroy local public education than Federal interference with education. This decision, and many others which followed, destroyed the right of local self-government as it relates to public education.

The current system of rule by elites in Washington, DC, will never change unless "We the people" decide we have had enough!

If we remain silent and accept the current political system — we will remain political slaves to our ruling elites. The time has come for a peaceful, non-violent Slave Revolt!

Chapter 6

The President no Longer Represents Average Americans

The power of America's neo-Marxist ruling elites[24] to control the president was demonstrated by their unrelenting scheming and near, if not actual, criminal actions against President Trump. President Trump had the support of America's middle-class. For the first time in modern history, the ruling elites were faced with a popularly elected president who did not owe his election to the elites. America's ruling elites were faced with a President who vowed to use his office to "drain the swamp" in Washington, DC. The elites were faced with a president who did not have their interests at heart — a president who vowed to make the interest of average Americans his primary concern. This, of course, meant he would not be part of their sinister and corrupt rule over "We the people." He threatened the federal perks, privileges, power, and profits they enjoy as America's ruling elite. Trump's election was a significant challenge for America's ruling elites. It meant that, to keep their positions of perks, privileges, power, and profits, the ruling elites had

In the current system of government, we do not elect a president for the American people, we elect a presidential placeholder who is used by neo-Marxist ruling elites in Washington, DC. We shall reclaim the right of local self-government and thereby change their government into our government!

to remove (impeach and convict) a president who the American people elected honestly and fairly. If they could not remove him via impeachment, then at least they had to destroy the president's ability to carry out his "America First" agenda.[25] This would be no problem for the ruling elite because they are specialists in political intrigue, and they proved it! Without realizing it, they also proved that Washington, DC, does not belong to the people — it belongs to the ruling elite. "We the people" are not citizens in a free Republic; we are subjects to our political masters in Washington, DC. "We the people" are actually nothing less than political slaves.

"We the people" do not elect a president for the American people — we elect a presidential placeholder who will protect and promote the ruling elite's power and privileges. If we manage to elect a president who will promote our interests, the ruling elite will nullify the election or, at least, use the Deep State's bureaucracy to block and attack the president's agenda during his short tenure in office. This has been the case since at least 1964. Modern American political history is a legacy of America's ruling elite using the power of government to enrich themselves and, also, enrich their political and social allies.

In 1969, Richard Nixon became the 37th President of the United States. He was elected using a Southern Strategy in which he proclaimed his devotion to traditional conservative American values. This upset the liberal left, especially the NAACP. After conservative Americans elected Nixon, he sent his future Attorney General, John Mitchell, to the NAACP and told them, "Watch what we do, not what we say." What followed was a flood of oppressive federal rules, regulations, and new agencies that focused on affirmative action (today labeled "diversity" or "equity"), the destruction of local public schools via

Freedom Now: A Non-Violent Conservative Revolution

bussing to achieve Federal Government mandated racial balance, and environmental activism. "We the people" elected Nixon, but after his election, he worked for the benefit of the ruling elite. However, as Nixon found out, doing the bidding of the ruling elite will not protect you from the left-of-center ruling elite.

Nixon's Watergate was minor compared to what the ruling elite did to President Trump, but the ruling elite get to decide which crimes to prosecute and which ones to ignore. They prosecute if it advances their neo-Marxist agenda, and they ignore it when it helps promote their agenda. "We the people" must obey the laws the elite decide to inflict upon us, but the ruling elite will always exempt themselves or their allies from the law if necessary to promote their neo-Marxist agenda.

In 1981, "We the people" elected Mr. Conservative Ronald Reagan as our president. While he waged a successful "Cold War" against the Soviet Union, his domestic policies did nothing to reverse decades of America's "progressive" movement toward an immoral and socialist society. He, like Nixon, campaigned in the South as a strong "States Rights" man. But in reality, he could do nothing to remove the unconstitutional concentration of political power in Washington, DC. Even Mr. Conservative Ronald Reagan was unable to stop the growth of big government, and he did nothing to stop America's immoral "slouch toward Gomorrah." "We the people" heard a lot of inspiring speeches during the Reagan years, but the framework of big government, a supreme Federal Government that is unaccountable to "We the people," was left in place ready to be used by the next president. The ruling elite in the Deep State merely "hunkered-down" and waited until a more pliable president took office after Reagan's two terms were completed.

In 1989, George W. H. Bush (the senior Bush) was elected president. He was Vice President under conservative Ronald Reagan and was presumed to be an honest conservative. He gained conservative votes by pledging that, under his administration, there would be "no new taxes." While campaigning for conservative votes, he boldly proclaimed, "Read my lips! No new taxes." Shortly after his election, he "compromised" with liberal Democrats and counterfeit-conservative Republicans and raised taxes. "We the people" get lip service, and the left gets more of our money while driving jobs out of the country.

In 2001, George W. Bush (George W. H. Bush's son) was elected president.[26] He was the anointed standard-bearer for the conservative cause. During his presidential campaign, he blasted the Clinton administration and Al Gore (Clinton's VP) for wasting money and American lives in their effort of "nation-building." Shortly after the terrorist attack of 9/11, Bush became an ardent advocate of "nation-building" as he engaged America in a number of no-win wars. Bush's dream was to turn the authoritarian governments of the mid-east into little democracies. He used American blood and treasure to force democracy on people who never in their entire history expressed any desire to establish democratic institutions. He had an unrealistic vision of turning tribal people into a democratic people. As an elitist, he never understood that democracy is not for every tribal people on earth. Democracy must develop over time from the bottom up — it cannot be forced upon a tribal people from the top down. It especially cannot be forced upon a people by an outside force — an outside force with an entirely different historical, cultural, ethnic, and religious background. One would think the elites would learn this from the disaster they gave us in Vietnam. American presidents of recent times gave the world endless, no-win wars. American taxpayers paid for these wars while the military-industrial complex gained enormous profits. "We the people" pay the taxes while mournfully greeting flag-draped coffins and watching while many veterans are homeless, and "our" government uses our taxes to take special care of illegal aliens.

This unacceptable system of rule over America's middle-class will remain if we continue to play "their" game of business-as-usual politics. And remember, their game is refereed by judges they hire and pay! We now have the tactics and a strategy to peacefully overthrow their unconstitutional rule. It is up to us to use irregular political warfare to restore local self-government and a legitimate constitutional Republic of Sovereign States.

It does not matter who we elect president IF there is not a fundamental change in the power structure in Washington, DC. The ruling elite will always protect their interests. It is time "We the people" had a government that will protect and promote our interests

Chapter 7

The Republican Party Does Not Represent Average Americans

The Republican Party, as far as average conservative Americans are concerned, is a Party of failure. For example, the GOP repeatedly failed to deliver on its promise to roll back Obamacare. Evidently, the Republican Party has more in common with the elites in Washington, DC, than with America's conservative voters. Conservatives began to question whether the GOP was sincere in its many pledges to support conservative values shortly after the election of Barack Obama as president (2008) and the GOP securing control of the House of Representatives two years later (2010). Popular displeasure of Obama's neo-Marxist Healthcare Act and increasing taxes caused an outpouring of American dissent expressed in numerous Tea Party rallies and marches nationwide. During this time, conservative Americans were given lip-service by "conservative" politicians but no real results — a lot of talk but no action. During this time, the Republican Party demonstrated the sad fact that it was a

The Republican Party is an essential part of the political establishment. The Republican Party will do nothing that would fundamentally upset or change the system of perks, privileges, power, and profits available to those holding elected office in Washington, DC. It is up to us to make a fundamental change in American politics.

key part of America's political status quo. America's political establishment is centered in Washington, DC, and is based upon the powers of an unconstitutional supreme Federal Government. The Republican Party is an essential part of the political establishment. The Republican Party will do nothing which would **fundamentally** upset or change the system of perks, privileges, power, and profits available to those holding elected office in Washington, DC. The Republican Party plays an essential role in protecting the Deep State! The Deep State could not exist without the Republican Party's support — all done, of course, quietly, behind the scenes, without the knowledge and understanding of America's conservative voters.

The Last Vote theory explains why the GOP can afford to betray conservatives

The reason the Republican Party's leadership can take "We the people" for granted is that they know conservatives have no realistic alternative other than voting for the Republican Party. They know conservatives will not vote for the liberal (actually neo-Marxist) Democrat candidate, and therefore, conservatives have no place to go other than the Republican Party. Some have suggested a third party, but such efforts have had limited success. In 1973, George Wallace established the American Independent Party, but it faded away after a "lone gunman" shot Wallace. In 1995, multi-millionaire Ross Perot founded the Reform Party, but it also faded away after Perot lost interest in politics. Other third parties have been around for decades, but they have no real impact on America's neo-Marxist political establishment.

The Republican Party's leadership understands that conservatives have no real choice. Conservatives who want

Freedom Now: A Non-Violent Conservative Revolution

to participate in America's electoral process must choose between liberal (neo-Marxist) Democrats or ineffective "conservative" Republicans. Two legal scholars summed up the thinking of Republican leadership:

"The conservatives had no place to go, they had to vote for you (the Republican candidate). So, give them (conservatives) some rhetoric to keep them happy. Push your real policies for the last vote. Where is the last vote? It is right next to the Democratic position on any issue. So, you adopt actual policies which get as close to the Democrats as you possibly can." [27]

An editorial in a 1993 issue of *The Wall Street Journal* quoted an Oklahoma Republican congressman explaining how things work in Washington, DC. When asked how he could continue getting reelected in such a conservative state while voting with the liberal majority — he explained:

"All you have to do is vote with the liberal leadership, and then make conservative press releases for your constituents to read." [28]

This is how "things are done" in Washington, DC's Deep State! This is how conservative Americans are, in effect, disenfranchised (abandoned) by our "conservative" leaders! In reality, under the current political establishment (the supreme Federal Government), our votes don't really matter. All our votes do is help maintain the status quo political establishment. No elected conservatives are able or even willing to attempt to make a *fundamental* change in the current system of unconstitutional supreme Federalism. When we elected Mr. Conservative Ronald Reagan president, he could not to make a *fundamental* change in America's political status quo. He managed to slow the growth of big government for a short while, but he did not reverse it, and as soon as he was gone, big government became even bigger and more oppressive. The same was true when Trump was elected president. No *fundamental* change was made, and as soon as he was gone, Federal tyranny became standard for all Americans

GOP Betrayal 2017 to 2022

In a 2017 article, outspoken columnist, Ann Coulter, blasted the Republican Party for its failure to fund Trump's pledge to "build the wall." She declared, "If this is the budget deal we get when Republicans control the House, the Senate, and the Presidency, there's no point in ever voting for a Republican again."[29]

Shortly after the 2017 shooting at the Congressional Baseball game in Alexandria, Virginia, a Republican Congressman from South Carolina declared that Trump was partially responsible for the shooting! Representative Sanford (R-SC) claimed Trump was a major cause of the toxic climate that inspired the shooter. Sanford declared, "I would argue that the president is at least partially … (to) blame for demons that have been unleashed."[30] This is the type of Republicans who make the job of the neo-Marxists in the media and politics so much easier.

There is a reason that the leadership of the GOP is grooming former South Carolina Governor Nikki Haley for a position as a future Presidential or Vice-Presidential candidate. Haley is a loyal establishment politician. Trump, in one of his many ill-thought-out, poor appointments, made her his representative to the United Nations (UN). Her close ties with the "Never Trump" movement were detailed in an article published in 2018. The article noted:

United Nations Deputy Ambassador Jon Lerner has deep ties to not only his longtime colleague and boss, U.N. Ambassador Nikki Haley, but also Facebook CEO Mark Zuckerberg, the failed "Never Trump" movement, and the pro-mass immigration billionaire GOP mega-donors the Koch brothers.[31]

Nikki Haley is a prime example of elected Republicans who eagerly turn their backs on conservative voters while supporting the Deep State, the ruling elite, and GOP Chamber of Commerce big money boys. Southerners should never forget that Nikki Haley initiated the anti-Confederate monument movement while Governor of South Carolina. While she proudly displays her foreign (India) heritage, she, by her actions as Governor, shamefully slandered Southern heritage as being racist and needing to be removed from America. She represents her self-interest while cozying up to the ruling elites who look to her as a potential presidential or vice-presidential candidate. With Republicans like Nikki Haley — who needs Democrats?

Politicians in leadership roles in the Republican Party are not beyond lying to conservative voters to get elected. Hypocrisy is no barrier to an aspiring politician. One day, they will support a neo-Marxist cause — the removal of an historical monument that just one person claims it "offends" them — and then, while campaigning back home for reelection, they will change and suddenly become a loyal proponent of traditional American values. For example, a 2021 Republican candidate for Congress in Virginia was called out for making such a change:

Establishment Republican Jen Kiggans is campaigning for Congress on parental rights in education after voting with Democrats to cause Virginia's school crisis in the first place, forcing districts to open girl's rest-

rooms up to men and adopt "trans-affirming" policies under the Virginia Values Act.[32]

This is typical of what happens all across America — counterfeit conservatives betraying the goodwill and trust of conservative voters.

During the Chinese Communist initiated COVID pandemic, Republicans worked with Democrats to enforce tyrannical business and religious services shutdowns. Republicans even worked with Democrats to promote the establishment of a federal database to monitor who has or has not "voluntarily" received their COVID vaccination. Eighty Republicans voted to fund the establishment of the database. It is strange how the elite can find a "right to privacy" to justify abortion but cannot find a right to privacy when it comes to the NSA, CIA, or FBI collecting and monitoring our private phone calls or another government invasion of our privacy. An article published in 2021 names the Republicans who conspired with Democrats to develop a public monitoring database:

Eighty House Republicans voted with Democrats on Tuesday to pass the Immunization Infrastructure Modernization Act, which if passed by the Senate and signed into law would fund a federal vaccination database.[33]

The Republican Party is an expert in "voting counting" in Congress to determine just how many Republican votes are needed to pass liberal Democratic (neo-Marxist) legislation. Once the number of Republican votes needed is determined, the Republican leadership then allow Republicans in the more conservative districts or those facing a difficult reelection within the next few months to vote against the liberal legislation — while other moderate Republicans vote with the liberal majority. Thus, Congressional "conservatives" facing reelection can go back home and brag about voting against liberal legislation while the Republican Party actually facilitated the passage of liberal legislation. This is what Republican leaders in Washington and within our states mean when they tell us how important it is to "reach across the aisle and compromise with moderate Democrats." It is betrayal, pure and simple. Betrayal of America's Constitutional Republic of Sovereign States is an integral part of the Republican Party's political DNA. Under the current system of supreme federalism, the Republican Party is incapable of solving the very problem it created.[34]

The Republican Party's primary purpose is to maintain the political status quo. "We the people" must organize as a political pressure group and by conducting irregular political warfare, force a fundamental change in America's political establishment.

Chapter 8

The Solution — Abolishing Political Slavery via Local Self-Government and Real States' Rights

If we are to regain our right to local self-government, if we are to remove America's political ruling elites from their positions of perks, privileges, power, and profits, then we must turn our words into action. As explained in the Introduction, we are at a point where we face the potential of freedom. If we are to turn this potential into reality, we must be willing to face this awesome potential with truth and courage. How do we turn this vision of a new, constitutionally limited Federal Republic of Sovereign States that champions local self-government into an unstoppable mass movement?

Four Steps to Creating our Mass Movement for Freedom

Below are four essential steps we must take if we want to remove America's neo-Marxist ruling elites from their unconstitutional, and therefore illegitimate, positions of power in Washington, DC. These four steps will enable "We the people" to initiate a non-violent, conservative revolution which will destroy the influence/control our neo-Marxist enemies now have within our local communities, state, and society: [35]

1. We must elect *one of our own* to a statewide political office. This individual will then use his office as a Bully Pulpit to promote our Cause first in the South and then across the nation.

2. We must conduct irregular political warfare in which the goal is not necessarily to win elections but to inspire and motivate middle-class Americans to support our Cause actively. We will also use irregular political warfare to pressure "conservative" elected officials to support and promote our struggle to reclaim true American freedom, especially local self-government.

3. We must organize Provisional governments (shadow or parallel governments) in every Red County and Red State in America. We will use Provisional governments to support our lobbying efforts in state legislatures, counties, local municipalities, and school boards.

4. In those states that allow ballot initiatives, we will use our Provisional governments to establish a ballot initiative calling for the enactment of our Sovereign State Constitutional Amendment. [36] This Amendment to the U.S. Constitution will acknowledge the Sovereign State's right of nullification and secession. Political power will then be removed from Washington, DC, and returned to "We the people" of the Sovereign States. "We the people" will no longer fear the government, but the government will fear the people because we will, once again, hold the ultimate political power in our country!

The Bully Pulpit

For a movement to be successful, it needs a spokesperson who actively promotes the movement and, by virtue of his political standing, gives the movement credibility in the eyes of the general public. Teddy Roosevelt's Bull Moose Party is an example of a politician using his political office and prestige to promote a movement. Huey

Long and George Wallace are examples of other politicians who created movements. Ross Perot and Donald Trump used their enormous wealth and well-known social standing to create political movements. The problem with these movements is that they were centered around one person. Their movements were more like a personality cult. When they were no longer willing or were unable to carry on the struggle, then the movement died. For a movement to be successful over time, the person in the Bully Pulpit must promote the cause, not his political agenda.

Who Do We Trust to Fill the Bully Pulpit?

The individual in the Bully Pulpit must be "one of us." The person must be someone who is not a career politician, someone who will spend his time advancing the Cause, NOT his political career. The individual must understand the necessity of using irregular political warfare to unseat the political establishment. American values voters must begin to work together to raise the money necessary to contest and win a statewide office, select the targeted office, select the correct individual to fill the office, and then flood the state with volunteers to help elect "our" candidate. To ensure a successful campaign, the state should be well on the way to having an organized Provisional government in place before the election.

The Bully Pulpit — What Is It?

As explained in *Dixie Rising-Rules for Rebels*, the Bully Pulpit is a state-wide elected office in which the incumbent uses the prestige of the office to advance the Cause of American Constitutional liberty. The Bully Pulpit's officeholder will work with Provisional governments in each state to encourage the ratification of our Sovereign State Amendment or, if necessary, Red State — Red County secession and the establishment of a country of our own.[37] The office-holder in the Bully Pulpit becomes the spokesman for the Cause, not only in his state, but across the South and the nation. He is central to organizing and motivating pro-liberty folks in every Southern state and other Red States and Red Counties in non-Southern states. By virtue of his office, he generates public interest, knowledge, acceptance, and enthusiasm for our Cause.

The Bully Pulpit — Why Do We Need It?

The destruction of our Christian, conservative, American, and Southern heritage is not due to a lack of pro-Southern, pro-American values, books, blogs, or scholarly lectures. America's neo-Marxist enemies, slowly over time, infiltrated and captured the political establishment. They are now using it to destroy traditional Southern and American values. Only power can counter power. Currently, they have power, but we do not! One person in a Bully Pulpit could arouse the general public to support and engage in active and effective irregular political warfare. Southerners and other Americans will follow a strong leader who uses his Bully Pulpit to organize a mass movement; a leader who has developed a strategic plan to defeat the neo-Marxist mobs and replace the current illegitimate, supreme Federal Government with a Constitutional Republic of Sovereign States; and a leader who has a strategic plan to secure Constitutional rights by reclaiming real States' Rights inclusive of the rights of state nullification and secession. "We the people" must develop the mechanism to enforce the protections enumerated in the

Constitution. Always remember that the Constitution is not self-enforcing. By using irregular political warfare, establishing Provisional governments, and capturing a Bully Pulpit, we can create the power to enforce the limitations imposed on the Federal Government by the Constitution or, if necessary, create a nation of our own — a nation that protects and promotes traditional American values.

Irregular Political Warfare

As explained in *Dixie Rising-Rules for Rebels*, irregular political warfare is used by a smaller group fighting to throw-off the oppressive rule of a stronger political force. It is the opposite of "business-as-usual" politics. It is a strategic plan by which "We the people" can do an end-run around or out-flank the ruling elites in Washington, DC. As a smaller group, we may not elect our own people initially, but we can make sure that those who betray our trust face recall elections or are defeated in the next election. If, for example, a counterfeit conservative betrays us in the state legislature, we may well work with his Democratic opponent in the next election, causing the counterfeit conservative to lose his elected office. While this may seem unthinkable to those conducting business-as-usual politics, it is an excellent example of irregular political warfare. It is better to have a known opponent (who owes his election to you) at your front than to have a pretended friend "watching" your back. We must position ourselves to allow us to punish those who dare to betray our interests and values. ***All we have to do is defeat one or two counterfeit conservatives who betray us, and the entire herd will get the message.*** Soon, our so-called friends holding elected offices will begin to fear us! For the first time, "our" elected officials will face an organized, American-values, political group looking at the long-run (strategic) impact of our actions while counterfeit conservatives spend their time and effort looking at the next election's short-run impact on their personal political career. Their aim has always been to get elected and win re-election, while our aim is to secure for ourselves and generations to come, the American right of local self-government in an American Republic of Sovereign States.

Two keys to successful, irregular political warfare are (1) the Bully Pulpit, having at least *one statewide elected official in a Bully Pulpit and use him to help establish,* (2) Provisional governments in every Southern and non-Southern American values state and in every American-values counties (Red Counties) in neo-Marxists controlled Blue States.

Provisional State Governments

Provisional government, as used herein, is an organized group of individuals holding traditional, conservative, political, and moral values who work together to bring political pressure on elected officials to encourage them to protect and promote traditional American values. The Provisional government in each state operates as a lobbying effort to kill bad legislation and encourage the passage of legislation that will further our Cause. Our lobbying effort must start at the local level and not merely depend upon lobbyists in the state legislature. The Provisional government will be similar to the Tea Party movement. Still, unlike the failed Tea Party movement, our Provisional governments will be a movement which exercises real political clout guided by a strategic plan for ultimate victory. It uses various forms of public information to educate the public about the necessity of standing

Freedom Now: A Non-Violent Conservative Revolution

firm against America's neo-Marxist enemies. It will also educate the public about the virtue of and necessity for reclaiming our Constitutional rights of nullification and secession. Provisional governments in each state serve as the counter-balance to the evil, politically correct, Woke, leftist groups that currently control America. Our Provisional government is the organization that we will use to compel a *fundamental* change in the way "We the people" control our Federal Government.

Provisional governments in each state have three primary purposes:

1. Educate and arouse the public through a state-wide public relations campaign via social media, radio ads, and local meetings/rallies,
2. Lobby state legislature to defeat legislation that poses a threat to American values and enact legislation that supports traditional, conservative American values, and
3. Promote South-wide and non-Southern Red State ballot initiative, demanding passage of our Sovereign State Amendment to the U.S. Constitution. [38]

Provisional governments in each state take the place of spending enormous amounts of money running "our" candidates for elected office. Instead of trying to elect a majority of the members of the state legislature, we will use our Provisional government to influence the killing of harmful or passing of helpful legislation. We do not spend enormous amounts of scarce resources in an endless and usually fruitless effort to gain political office. Instead, we organize a Provisional government to influence (pressure) elected officials in the state legislature to vote against legislation harmful to our American and Southern values. Key to the success of our movement is to eventually enact legislation necessary to place our Sovereign State Amendment before the people of our state(s) via a state-wide ballot initiative. In the meantime, we continue to "educate to motivate" the general public, slowly turning them from passive conservatives into first, supporters and, eventually, active voters and workers for the Cause of regaining a Constitutionally limited Republic of Sovereign States. This is the essential work of irregular political warriors. We use the political system, but we do not become part of the political system. We do not engage our political enemies in a traditional political campaign. We do not engage in the traditional election cycle. Instead, we find opportunities to unite behind our select candidate — we carefully select one state-wide office for which we will run one of our own. This is a limited but *strategic* move to secure for our movement a "Bully Pulpit," first, in one state and then, in other "Red States."

Conducting Irregular Political Warfare in State Legislatures

While the national aim of our Provisional governments is to pursue the submission to the states and eventual ratification of our Sovereign State Amendment to the U.S. Constitution, we will also purse numerous legislative initiatives in state legislatures. We will encourage "conservative" legislators to introduce legislation that would benefit the cause of preserving and promoting traditional American values. For example, we will introduce riders to bills providing tax revenues for public universities, requiring them to allow academic credits for attending university-sponsored lectures, promoting traditional American values, and providing harsh punishment for students, faculty, or outsiders who attempt to disrupt these lectures. Conservative speech will be protected in all universities and other educational institutions financed by America's taxpayers. We will introduce legislation defining "racism" as the advocating of using racial distinctions to deny equal rights under the law. If anyone accuses an individual of being a racist, etc., but cannot provide clear evidence that the individual labeled as a racist [39] meets the statutory definition of a racist, then the accuser will be guilty of slander, and also, such slander will be treated as a hate crime. We will also seek new laws requiring strict enforcement of voter identification and the policing of voter registration rolls. Individuals, elected or appointed, who are responsible for maintaining the integrity of voting will be personally liable to class action suits by aggrieved voters to determine if they intentionally or negligently failed to perform their duties to maintain the integrity of the State's voting system.

As with all politicians, state legislators respond to pressure, especially from their local constituents. This is why the Provisional government must spend a great deal of time and effort explaining and promoting our cause at the local level via radio, newspaper, and social media advertisements. An American-values lobbyist in the state legislature is useless without back-up in local counties. People at the local level must understand what we are doing in the state's legislature and why we are doing it. They must feel that they are a part of the movement to restore true, conservative, American values. As explained in *Dixie Rising-Rules for Rebels*, we must first educate our fellow Americans and then turn them into supporters and eventually into activists fighting to reclaim our country or, *if necessary,* create a Red State — Red County nation of our own.

Freedom Now: A Non-Violent Conservative Revolution

Concluding Comments

Traditional business-as-usual politics created a nation controlled by liberals who are advocates of a neo-Marxist (Woke, politically correct) view of society. The left-of-center political class is aided and abetted by counterfeit conservatives who never expressed an interest in returning ultimate political power to "We the people" at the local level. Traditional business-as-usual politics will not solve the very problems it created. The cause of Freedom is too important to leave up to the "good-will" of elected politicians. If Freedom is to be restored to America, it must be restored by people working at the local level using irregular political warfare.

The cliches of liberalism and the false promises of counterfeit conservatives are at war with the spiritual values and religious faith that form the base of the family and community. Liberals (actually neo-Marxist) sing their siren songs, promising to perfect an imperfect man. Meanwhile, there is no emphasis on spiritual values by counterfeit-conservatives based in Washington, DC. Present-day conservatism stresses the value of the material while ignoring the value of the spirit. Little thought is given to culture, family, or community — what Southerners of old called our kith-and-kin. There is only talk of next month's economic indicators, unemployment numbers, interest rates, or the possibilities awaiting next year's election. It is crass materialistic politics devoid of the spiritual values necessary to maintain a free, happy, and prosperous people.

"We the people" can correct America's neo-Marxist slouch toward socialism, and Gomorrah! But, do we have the will and courage to do it?

Deo Vindice!

Freedom Now: A Non-Violent Conservative Revolution

Endnotes

1 This includes the lower Federal Courts and Administrative Agencies such as the Internal Revenue Service (IRS), Equal Employment Opportunities Commission (EEOC), Environmental Protection Agency (EPA), and most recently, the upper echelons of the "Woke" military.

2 America's "moral" values are based upon the Bible's "Golden Rule" that instructs us to "Do unto others as ye would have them do unto you." We will no longer allow the neo-Marxists to force us to live according to their perverted standards, and in the same vein, we will not force them to live under our standards. For example, If the people of a leftist, neo-Marxist controlled state want to allow men who identify as women to compete in sports against biological females, then that is their business, but we will not allow them to use the force of government to compel us to accept their perverted social standards. This is the beauty of local self-government. Local self-government allows each society to govern itself according to the will (consent) of the people within that state or local community as allowed by that state.

3 The proletariat is the social class of wage-earners, those members of a society whose only possession of significant economic value is their labor, their capacity to work. Marx considered the proletariat to be exploited by rich capitalists (the bourgeoisie), and forced to accept meager wages with no hope of economic or social mobility.

4 Hicks, Stephen R. C., *Explaining Postmodernism* (2004, Connor Court Publishing, Redland Bay, QLD, 2019), 1, 21, & 171.

5 The white patriarchy, as described by postmodernists and other neo-Marxists, is a system of society or government in which white men hold the power, while women and others, such as blacks, homosexuals, or illegal immigrants are powerless and are exploited by the "evil" patriarchy.

6 Instead of rejecting their failed system of communism and socialism, neo-Marxists merely reinvented it and as postmodernists, seized control of America's educational system of higher learning. They turned America's universities and other educational institutions, kindergarten through high school, into anti-traditional, American values indoctrination centers. The 2020 riotous mobs in America's streets are evidence of the success of their left-of-center indoctrination of America's youth, paid for

by America's God-fearing, middle-class taxpayers.

7 The exact quote reads: "… the palpable truth that the mass of mankind has not been born, with saddles on their backs, nor a favored few booted and spurred, ready to ride them legitimately, by the grace of god." https://tjrs.monticello.org/letter/443 accessed 2/22/2022.

8 The destruction of the original constitutional Republic of Sovereign States and the creation of the unconstitutional supreme Federal Government is discussed in detail in Kennedy & Kennedy, *The South Was Right!* 3rd edition (1991, 1994, Shotwell Publishing, Columbia, SC: 2020).

9 As cited in, Colbourn, Trevor, *The Lamp of Experience* (Liberty Fund, Indianapolis, Indiana: 1965), 189.

10 As cited in, Colbourn, Trevor, *The Lamp of Experience* (Liberty Fund, Indianapolis, Indiana: 1965), 132.

11 www.opensecrets.org/news/2020/04/majority-of-lawmakers-millionaires/ accessed 2/24/2022.

12 McCarthy, Andrew C., *Ball of Collusion-The plot To Rig an Election and Destroy a Presidency* (Encounter Books, NY: 2019), 40.

13 www.breitbart.com/politics/2022/01/26/schweizer-pelosi-wont-allow-hearings-on-covid-origin-while-her-family-does-a-lot-of-business-in-china/ accessed 1/27/2022.

14 www.breitbart.com/politics/2022/01/31/red-handed-23-former-u-s-senators-and-congressmen-who-lobby-for-chinese-military-or-chinese-intelligence-linked-companies/ accessed 2/1/2022.

15 www.redvoicemedia.com/2021/11/21-house-republicans-push-to-make-transgenders-a-federally-protected-class/ accessed 11/24/2021.

16 www.breitbart.com/radio/2020/06/15/carrie-severino-scotus-lgbt-decision-tsunami-litigation-religious-groups/ accessed 6/16/2020.

17 www.law.uchicago.edu/news/adam-chilton-examines-political-leanings-legal-scholars accessed 3/2/2022.

18 www.churchmilitant.com/news/article/transgender-rapist-gets-free-sex-change 12/31/2020.

19 www.nationalreview.com/2015/02/how-epa-wants-use-river-regulations-regulate-farmers-andrew-langer/ accessed 6/5/2020.

20 http://news.trust.org/item/20190627144409-81k6q accessed 6/27/2019.

21 www.breitbart.com/news/judge-orders-release-of-migrants-in-florida-as-virus-measure/ accessed 5/4/2020.

22 www.breitbart.com/politics/2020/05/29/chief-justice-john-roberts-sides-with-liberal-justices-as-supreme-court-rules-in-favor-of-restrictions-on-religious-services/ accessed 5/30/2020.

23 www.history.com/this-day-in-history/supreme-court-declares-desegregation-busing-constitutional-swann-v-charlotte-mecklenburg accessed 3/3/2022.

24 America's ruling elites are a loosely affiliated group of politicians from both political parties, Deep State bureaucrats, Wall Street financial elites, well-paid corporate lobbyists, and their allies in the mainline and digital media, and leftists who control America's educational system. They all accept, if not actively support, a neo-Marxist social/political ideology.

25 Senator Rand Paul noted that the Deep State was working to destroy the elected president, "FBI Mistress, Lisa Page, confirmed to House Judiciary, there was an anti-Trump Insurance Policy and it's the fake Russian investigation!" Cited in, www.washingtonpost.com/politics/2019/03/14/what-strzok-page-insurance-policy-text-was-actually-about/ accessed 4/12/2022.

26 He is the president who called Islam the religion of peace. https://georgewbush-whitehouse.archives.gov/news/releases/2001/09/20010917-11.html accessed 4/12/2022.

27 William J. Quirk & Randall R. Bridwell, as cited in Kennedy & Kennedy, *Why Not Freedom* (Pelican Publishing Co., Gretna, LA: 1995), 51.

28 As cited in Kennedy & Kennedy, *Why Not Freedom* (Pelican Publishing Co., Gretna, LA: 1995), 246.

29 Ann Coulter: Swamp People: 47; Trump: 0 www.breitbart.com/big-government/2017/05/03/ann-coulter-swamp-people-47-trump-0/ accessed 5/4/2017.

30 www.breitbart.com/clips/2017/06/15/gop-rep-sanford-trump-partially-blame-environment-led-alexandria-shooting/ accessed June 15, 2017.

31 www.breitbart.com/big-government/2018/04/17/nikki-haleys-deputy-ambassador-led-never-trump-movement-launched-zuckerbergs-open-borders-group/ accessed 4/18/2018.

32 nationalfile.com/virginia-kiggans-voted-dems-trans-school-bathrooms-now-campaigns-parental-rights-schools/ accessed 12/23/2021.

33 www.breitbart.com/politics/2021/12/01/exclusive-tool-to-enforce-orwellian-rules-80-house-republicans-help-pass-bill-to-fund-federal-vaccination-database/ accessed 12/2/2021.

34 For a full explanation of the Republican Party's role in creating the current system of unconstitutional supreme federalism, see Kennedy & Kennedy, *The South Was Right!* (1991, 1994, Shotwell Publishing Co., Columbia, SC: 2020), 219-66.

35 These four steps are more fully explained in Kennedy, James Ronald, *Dixie Rising-Rules for Rebels* 2nd ed. (2017, Shotwell Publishing, Columbia, SC: 2021).

36 Copy of the Sovereign State Constitution Amendment can be found in *Dixie Rising-Rules for Rebels*, 2nd edition, 117-21.

37 See, Kennedy, James Ronald, *Red State Red County Secession-Creating a Nation of Our Own* (The Scuppernong Press, Wake Forest, NC: 2020).

38 Copy of the Sovereign State Amendment to the U.S. Constitution can be found in *Dixie Rising-Rules for Rebels* 2nd ed., 117-21.

39 The label of racist includes other neo-Marxist "code words" used by the left such as "white supremacist."

Freedom Now: A Non-Violent Conservative Revolution

Books By Ron Kennedy

Freedom Now! A Non-Violent Conservative Revolution
Dixie Rising-Rules for Rebels
Red State-Red County Secession: Creating a Nation of Our Own
Be Ye Separate: Bible Belt Revival or Marxist Revolution
Nullifying Federal and State Gun Control
When Rebel Was Cool
Nullifying Tyranny
Nullification: Why and How
Uncle Seth Fought the Yankees

Books by the Kennedy Twins

The South Was Right!
Punished With Poverty: The Suffering South
Yankee Empire: Aggressive Abroad and Despotic at Home
Rawls View of the Constitution: Secession as Taught at West Point
Jefferson Davis: The High Road to Emancipation and Constitutional Government

Author's website: www.kennedytwins.com

Freedom Now: A Non-Violent Conservative Revolution

James Ronald (Ron) Kennedy

Ron Kennedy was born and raised in south central Mississippi. In 1974 he moved to Louisiana where he now resides.

Ron received a Master's in Health Administration (MHA) from Tulane University in New Orleans, a Master of Jurisprudence in Health Law (MJ) from Loyola University Chicago, a Bachelor's degree from Northeast Louisiana University. He retired in April 2015 after serving more than 20 years as Vice President of Risk Management for a Louisiana based insurance company.

Ron and his twin brother Donnie are the authors of the bestselling book *The South Was Right!* with more than 140,000 copies sold — the third updated edition was released in November of 2020. The Kennedy Twins have co-authored numerous other books including: *Punished with Poverty — the Suffering South*; and, *Yankee Empire: Aggressive Abroad and Despotic at Home.*

Ron's most recent books are: *Dixie Rising — Rules for Rebels, When Rebel Was Cool, Red State Red County Secession, Be Ye Separate-Bible Belt Revival or Marxist Revolution*, and *Nullifying Federal and State Gun Control.*

Ron is past Commander of the Louisiana Division Sons of Confederate Veterans. He is a frequent speaker at Southern Heritage and conservative meetings.

Author's website: www.kennedytwins.com